VERMIN

BY BENNY AINSWORTH

Published by Playdead Press 2023

© Benny Ainsworth 2023

Benny Ainsworth has asserted his rights under the Copyright, Design and Patents Act, 1988, to be identified as the author of this work.

A CIP catalogue record for this book is available from the British Library.

ISBN 978-1-915533-12-8

Caution

All rights whatsoever in this play are strictly reserved and application for performance should be sought through the author before rehearsals begin. No performance may be given unless a license has been obtained.

This book is sold subject to the condition that it shall not by way of trade or otherwise, be lent, resold, hired out, or otherwise circulated without the publisher's prior consent in any form of binding or cover other than that in which it is published and without a similar condition including this condition being imposed on the subsequent purchaser.

Playdead Press
www.playdeadpress.com

THE VENUE

Arcola Theatre was founded by Mehmet Ergen and Leyla Nazli in September 2000. Originally located in a former textile factory on Arcola Street in Dalston, in January 2011 the theatre moved to its current location in a former paint-manufacturing workshop on Ashwin Street. In 2021, we opened an additional outdoor performance space just around the corner from the main building: Arcola Outside.

Arcola Theatre produces daring, high-quality theatre in the heart of East London and beyond. We commission and premiere exciting, original works alongside rare gems of world drama and bold new productions of classics. Our socially engaged, international programme champions diversity, challenges the status quo, and attracts over 65,000 people to our building each year. Ticket prices are some of the most affordable in London.

Every year, we offer 26 weeks of free rehearsal space to culturally diverse and refugee artists; our Grimeborn Festival opens up opera with contemporary stagings at affordable prices; and our Participation department creates over 13,500 creative opportunities for the people of Hackney and beyond. Our pioneering environmental initiatives are award-winning and aim to make Arcola the world's first carbon-neutral theatre.

Arcola has won awards including the UK Theatre Award for Promotion of Diversity, The Stage Award for Sustainability and the Peter Brook Empty Space Award.

OUR TEAM

Artistic Director | Mehmet Ergen

Deputy Artistic Director | Leyla Nazli
& Executive Producer

Production Coordinator | Charlotte McShane

Marketing Coordinator | Millie Whittam

Branding and Digital Coordinator | Ashen Page

Finance Manager | Steve Haygreen

Participation Manager | Charlotte Croft

Chief Technician | Michael Paget

Sales Managers | Catriona Tait & Carmen Keeley Foster

Software Developer & IT Support | Oliver Brill

Facilities Maintenance | Niall Bateson

Cleaner | Milton Vargas Rodriguez

TRUSTEES

Andrew Cripps (Chair) Gabriel Gbadamosi
Naz Yeni (Vice Chair) Lynne McKenzie
Ben Todd Abdullah Tercanli

Arcola Theatre
24 Ashwin Street
London, E8 3DL

www.arcolatheatre.com

The REcreate Agency is a multidisciplinary creative agency that develops the potential in independent artists, producers and projects.

Founded in 2020 by independent producers Reece McMahon and Emily Beecher, **REcreate** exists to facilitate freelance artists to not only make work but to think about what they need to make their best work. With over 22 years combined experience working as freelancers, in organisations, institutions and in commercial and subsidised settings, we support artists to rethink their approach to creation and value their own artistic development and self-care as much as the projects they work so hard to develop.

REcreate is led and managed by Reece & Emily, both of whom are artists and producers in their own right with direct connections to the UK's most prolific cultural organisations. We develop projects with people at the centre of them, generating and investing in opportunities that allow artists and producers to take risks, grow and learn 'on-the-job'.

REcreate is at the forefront of cultural change and is changing the culture of how we share, talk, and think about making work together.

The REcreate Agency is:

Reece McMahon – Co-Creative Director / Producer
Emily Beecher – Co-Creative Director / Producer
Bobby Harding – Associate Producer

www.recreate-agency.co.uk

 @recreate_agency   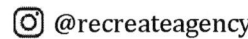 @recreateagency

TRIPTYCH THEATRE

Triptych Theatre was founded in 2014 by Sally Paffett, Benny Ainsworth and Michael Parker, at East 15 Acting School. Our mission is to raise a mirror to modern Britain through telling incredible stories designed to appeal to a modern generation of theatre-goers.

From the conception of the company, Triptych have dared to create fearless and challenging new writing which faces up to the darkest elements of human nature. Through performing our plays at fringe festivals, Triptych Theatre have succeeded in gaining a cult following, as well as numerous circuit awards, through bold concepts and sharp text. Triptych Theatre exclusively write, direct and perform our own plays.

Previous shows include *Scattered* and *An Audience with Stuart Bagcliffe*.

All co-founders, co-artistic directors, co-producers and close friends:

Sally Paffett

Benny Ainsworth

Michael Parker

This production of *Vermin* was first performed at the Arcola Theatre, London on 14th March 2023 with the following cast and creative:

RACHEL   **Sally Paffett**

BILLY   **Benny Ainsworth**

Director | **Michael Parker**

Writer | **Benny Ainsworth**

Lighting Designer | **Alex Lewer**

Sound Designer | **Ben Sorab**

Producer | **Reece McMahon & Emily Beecher for The REcreate Agency**

Associate Producer | **Bobby Harding for The REcreate Agency**

Publicist | **Storytelling PR**

Image credit | **Meurig Marshall**

Vermin premiered at the Edinburgh Fringe Festival 2022 at Gilded Balloon Teviot House from 3rd – 27th August 2022.

For D.

Hope you're something better than a rat.

CHARACTERS

Rachel

Billy

BILLY: It was quick.

RACHEL: By some people's standards, Bill –

BILLY: Well, the standards have shifted, haven't they?

RACHEL: I suppose you're right. He's right. They have.

BILLY: They really have.

RACHEL: What with tinder, bumble, you know, all these

BILLY: Most people just meet and skip the whole

RACHEL: The getting to know each other part –

BILLY: Yeah, and just fuck it out like animals.

RACHEL: We weren't like that.

BILLY: No, not that quick.

RACHEL: But still quick.

BILLY: We met on a train.

RACHEL: Quite romantic that, isn't it? Like the old days.

BILLY: The Southern service to Victoria from Carshalton Beeches was held at a red signal outside Balham for a good forty-five minutes.

RACHEL: Someone had killed themselves that day.

BILLY: Well, not yet, Rach.

RACHEL: No, not yet.

BILLY: He was lying down on the tracks in front of the train.

RACHEL: Refusing to move.

BILLY: So they called in police and a negotiator, I don't know if that's the right word –

RACHEL: A calmer-downer.

BILLY: A suicide stopper.

RACHEL: A negotiator – to reason with the guy –

BILLY: And we're sitting opposite each other in one of those bits with two seats either side of a table,

RACHEL: And the driver pipes up,

BILLY: Explains the situation.

RACHEL: It's always funny to see how people react to stuff like that.

BILLY: I heard a couple in the seats behind me saying "Oh God, that's awful", you know, "I hope he's alright".

RACHEL: And there was a fat 'Turkishy' looking businessman next to them who just huffed, looked at his watch and mumbled "for fuck's sake".

BILLY: That's when I clocked her.

RACHEL: I had climbed up on my seat to try and get a view out of the top bit of the window, see what was going on.

BILLY: See anything?

RACHEL: Not from here but the platform curves round. If I get forward a couple of carriages and try a window on the other side I might be able to see something.

BILLY: Got to be somewhere?

RACHEL: Not really – you?

BILLY: Just home.

RACHEL: Wanna have a look?

BILLY: So we clambered out of our seats and pass down the aisles –

RACHEL: Through the doors –

BILLY: To an open window on the right hand side of the train.

RACHEL: It's an early afternoon service so it isn't too busy –

BILLY: And the few people that are there are just buried in their phones,

RACHEL: Reading books.

BILLY: Not interested.

RACHEL: Bored.

BILLY: Yeah, we've been there a while by this point.

RACHEL: But we're not bored.

BILLY: No.

RACHEL: We're interested.

BILLY: Very.

RACHEL: Intrigued.

BILLY: Very intrigued.

RACHEL: And looking out the window we can see-

BILLY: Police –

RACHEL: Yeah, and –

BILLY: The calmer-downer –

RACHEL: Suicide stopper –

BILLY: There in a yellow high-vis.

RACHEL: Crouched down on the side of the platform with this earnest look on his face.

BILLY: I crane my neck a bit, to get a better view.

RACHEL: Can you see him?

BILLY: Yeah, I can see his head.

RACHEL: Move up.

BILLY: I shifted my body round.

RACHEL: And I push myself up on the chair.

BILLY: And she nuts me right in the chin. Nearly chipped a bloody tooth. Shit!

RACHEL: Fuck, I'm sorry.

BILLY: It's fine, really.

RACHEL: So I bob back up, more carefully this time-

BILLY: And I know this sounds weird –

RACHEL: It's cute, Bill.

BILLY: Cute but a bit weird.

RACHEL: My head was like, here, on him.

BILLY: I sniffed her hair. Fruity.

RACHEL: My conditioner.

BILLY: And she looks up at me, and I hadn't even noticed but you know what?

RACHEL: (*coyly*) What?

BILLY: She's actually really pretty.

RACHEL: It's great conditioner.

BILLY: She says, "I think it's worked".

RACHEL: He peers round.

BILLY: She was right, the man on the tracks was getting up.

RACHEL: And the negotiator had his hand stretched out

BILLY: And they're smiling at each other.

RACHEL: And crying.

BILLY: Smiling and crying.

RACHEL: And it's over.

BILLY: Trains start to move again around the station.

RACHEL: But not ours because they're still talking there –

BILLY: And the police and station staff are going over,

RACHEL: And they're all there having a jolly little chat,

BILLY: The man takes the negotiator's arm,

RACHEL: He heaves himself up onto the platform.

BILLY: And then –

RACHEL: From nowhere –

BILLY: No warning,

RACHEL: You tell this bit.

BILLY: He sprints across to platform three and leaps in front of the fast service to Epsom Downs and goes splat.

RACHEL: And we can't really see because of the way the platform's raised above the tracks.

BILLY: But we know he's dead,

RACHEL: Because one of the train wheels further back in the first carriage kicks up some guts onto the edge of the platform.

BILLY: Then the screaming starts,

RACHEL: Pitched against the screech of the train brakes,

BILLY: And the atmosphere is frantic for all of fifteen seconds.

RACHEL: And then just disbelief.

BILLY: Shock.

RACHEL: But not us.

BILLY: No, not us.

RACHEL: I look up at him

BILLY: And I look down at her

RACHEL: And there's something strange

BILLY: It's hard to describe

RACHEL: And

BILLY: We

RACHEL: Kiss.

BILLY: The most incredible kiss.

(*Pause*)

BILLY: And that's how we met.

RACHEL: Romantic, right?

BILLY: Like the old days.

RACHEL: Three months later Billy proposed.

BILLY: She said yes.

RACHEL: Of course I said yes.

BILLY: It was a bit of a whirlwind.

RACHEL: A bit?

BILLY: OK, a lot of a whirlwind.

RACHEL: We were that irritatingly loved up couple.

BILLY: Really hands on.

RACHEL: Oh God, so hands on.

BILLY: And chittering away constantly like little birds.

RACHEL: I'd heard of it, but never experienced love like that,

BILLY: The kind of love that takes over everything.

RACHEL: Four months after that we were married, and just over a year after that we decided to buy the flat.

BILLY: We'd been looking around a few places in the run-up to this.

RACHEL: We didn't have much of a budget, there were just a few things that had to be right.

BILLY: We wanted it to be South London.

RACHEL: We both grew up around there.

BILLY: Three bedrooms.

RACHEL: I was massive at the time.

BILLY: Not fat.

RACHEL: No, I was –

BILLY: She was –

RACHEL: We were pregnant, at the time.

BILLY: Well, I wasn't pregnant.

RACHEL: It's called a turn of phrase, Bill.

BILLY: It's called a joke, Rach.

RACHEL: He does that.

BILLY: She loves it really.

RACHEL: Hilarious. It didn't work out.

BILLY: The pregnancy.

RACHEL: It's very common.

BILLY: It happens a lot.

RACHEL: She was called Alice.

(*Beat*)

BILLY: So we had –

RACHEL: One room for our girl, for when she would have been a bit older, one for me and one for Billy. I need my own space when I sleep.

BILLY: I snore.

RACHEL: Somewhat.

BILLY: Anyway, we found the perfect place, just off the high street in Streatham Hill.

RACHEL: A three bedroom ground floor flat.

BILLY: It was a white box.

RACHEL: We saw a lot of potential there. Billy fancies himself a bit of a DIY whizz.

BILLY: Yeah, DIY, decorating, I like getting my hands dirty.

RACHEL: So we set about making it a home.

BILLY: It wasn't easy.

RACHEL: There were disputes.

BILLY: My fault, of course.

RACHEL: Not always.

BILLY: A lot of the time.

RACHEL: He was obsessed with building this little shed out the back for all his tools and other bits and bobs.

BILLY: Well, because they were just sitting in the corridor at this point.

RACHEL: That's true, but it became all consuming, three weeks or more spent making this weird little shed perfect.

BILLY: I'm quite an obsessive person about some things, I've got diagnosed OCD.

RACHEL: When he gets his heart set on an idea, it's impossible to stop him.

BILLY: It's a great shed.

RACHEL: It's the most well organised shed you've ever seen. Scores of these little labelled boxes at the back with all the smaller stuff and then rows of hooks, all different sizes lining the walls.

BILLY: That's where I keep my hand tools, the electric tools are in boxes stacked up at the back.

RACHEL: Anyway, eventually, after a bit of a struggle, I managed to divert his attention back to the house. It took a while, but we really got the place looking great.

BILLY: I did a good job.

RACHEL: You did.

BILLY: And one night we're sitting there in our newly completed, beautiful little flat, and we're having a glass of wine in the kitchen, suddenly we hear this noise.

RACHEL: Squeaking.

BILLY: Scratching.

RACHEL: Bodies moving around.

BILLY: Under the floorboards.

RACHEL: Mice?

BILLY: Big mice.

RACHEL: Rats.

BILLY: For fuck's sake. I'll get some traps tomorrow. Just make sure you don't leave any food out.

RACHEL: I remember thinking it's crazy how clearly we could hear them.

BILLY: We could track their routes around the space under the kitchen just by using our ears.

RACHEL: They had all these little pathways dug out. Sometimes you could hear them under the floor in the corridor, scratching frantically,

BILLY: Expanding their network.

RACHEL: Making something of a home for themselves.

BILLY: But this was our home,

RACHEL: Not theirs.

BILLY: The next day I went to Wilko's and bought ten large wooden traps.. the classic style, like the ones from the film Mousetrap, but bigger. I'd never dealt with rodents before but how hard could it be?

RACHEL: You'd dealt with other things before.

BILLY: That's true, actually.

RACHEL: Tell them.

BILLY: When I was a kid, I liked killing stuff.

RACHEL: It's actually very common, I googled it.

BILLY: Mainly insects, you know, stamping on ants, cutting worms in half, and half again. Sticking pins through beetles, you know, normal stuff.

RACHEL: Nothing weird.

BILLY: No.

RACHEL: Although there was the cat.

BILLY: Yeah, there was the cat.

RACHEL: Go on.

BILLY: When my mum found out about this one she made me stop, it was the last thing I killed. They don't need to hear it.

RACHEL: You can't just bring up the cat and then not tell the story.

BILLY: It wasn't me that brought up the cat, it was you.

RACHEL: Still...

BILLY: OK, but just remember, I was really young.

RACHEL: You were thirteen.

BILLY: That's young.

RACHEL: Tell it!

BILLY: There were loads of cats in the neighbourhood where I grew up. They'd roam through the back gardens on the street where we lived, suckering all of us into giving them little bits of food. They were fat, privileged little bastards. There was this pure white one, big and round, with a snooty little face and a large fluffy tail, we'll call him Jeff. I was in the garden, thirteen years old, remember, and I'd just killed my first bird. I'd tried before but it's hard to trick birds, they're clever, and they're fast. This time I'd been gifted it on a plate, it was as if on this occasion the universe had ruled it was time for Billy to move on from insects, to kill a bird.

RACHEL: Did you just refer to yourself in the third person?

BILLY: I'm telling the bloody story!

RACHEL: Keep going.

BILLY: It was injured, you see, I'm not sure how but its wing was askew, with feathers jutting out in all the wrong directions. It was just lying there flapping and rolling around. So I went inside to grab the keys to my dad's shed. My dad's shed was even better than mine is, and my shed is a fucking masterpiece. It was like Charlie and the Chocolate Factory, but with tools instead of sweets. There were hammers and screwdrivers in their hundreds, shovels, drills, pliers, hedge trimmers, garden hoes, trowels, you name it, it was all in there, all in its perfect place. How should I kill this bird? Should I take a screwdriver, and stab its eyes out? Maybe I should saw it in half lengthways. Or I could just bosh it into the ground with a sledgehammer, quick.

RACHEL: But he didn't use any of those.

BILLY: No, I didn't.

RACHEL: What did you do?

BILLY: I closed the shed door, and I locked it, put the keys in my pocket. This was my first bird. I didn't want it to be the same as the insects, you know, impersonal. I wanted to be as close to the action as possible. So I picked it up with my hands, and looked into its eyes as it writhed around, trying to free itself. (*beat*) I was surprised by how stringy it was. And how strong, come to think of it. It took a good thirty seconds for me to completely pull the head off, but the bird shut up as soon as the bones snapped. When I managed to break the skin it didn't bleed as much as I expected, but tendons, veins, muscles, I don't really know exactly which bit, stretched out from the disconnected head to the body, keeping it attached. And that's when Jeff turned up.

RACHEL: The cat.

BILLY: Yeah, they know.

RACHEL: Sorry.

BILLY: Anyway, Jeff reckoned it was dinner time. He comes over and quick as flash he takes up the dangling head in his mouth, now I'm playing tug of war with this fucking cat, there's feathers flying everywhere and neither of us are letting go. I remember I still have the keys to the shed in my pocket, so I keep hold of the bird with my right hand and fish out the keys with my left and then bam! Bam, bam, bam. Cat didn't see it coming. Four sharp stabs to the neck with these keys and it let go. Now the cat's there in front of me, bleeding... What do I do? Too late to drop it back off at the owner's house. Plus, a cat... that's one up on a bird, isn't it? I use the whole bunch of keys to smash it over the head one more time and it drops to the ground. I dash over to the shed, I've gotta think fast now, something quick, something efficient. Shears. I take the shears out and walk back over to the cat, who's lying there looking dazed, I put the shears over it's back left leg and close. Well if I'd been surprised by how little blood came out of the bird, it was shocking just how much came out of the cat. It came squirting out of the hole I made like a sprinkler, spraying all over the dead bird. It's moving around loads now, and making loads of noise. I grab it and the bastard scratches me right down my face but I don't walk away. No. I carefully, but forcefully place the shears over its other back leg and close. This one doesn't come off so easily, took a good few cracks to get it off completely because of how we were positioned. The other two legs were easy because the cat had given up. Then that stupid tail. It was left lying on the ground like a sad puff of candy floss. Mum found the legs the next day in the outside bin, that's how she learned about what had happened. As you can imagine I was quite severely reprimanded. Dad beat me 'til I bled. You look shocked. I was a kid! It was a long time ago.

RACHEL: I love that story.

BILLY: How many times have you heard it?

RACHEL: And I still love it.

BILLY: And you love animals, don't you Rach?

RACHEL: I do, but we're all suckers for violence aren't we, let's be honest. True crime on Netflix, eighties slasher horror flicks, we all love it.

BILLY: Not everyone babe, but we certainly do. I've forgotten what we were talking about.

RACHEL: The rats.

BILLY: Oh shit, that's right.

RACHEL: He's a goldfish.

BILLY: In short I had some limited experience in killing things. But these were traps, you know-

RACHEL: You just set them and walk away.

BILLY: How hard could that be?

RACHEL: As it turned out, very. Rats, if you don't know, are almost as intelligent as dogs.

BILLY: We followed all the advice, new bait once a week, mix up the diet on offer. The trouble was the local restaurants.

RACHEL: We'd find bits of naan on the floor,

BILLY: Rice,

RACHEL: The odd poppadom,

BILLY: Curry stuff, stuff we hadn't eaten. They had all the food they needed, and what we needed was a new strategy.

RACHEL: Billy was out buying some cement, we'd located a couple of holes on the outside of the house he could fill in with pretty little bother,

BILLY: I hadn't really used cement before so I considered it a bit of fun.

RACHEL: I was in the kitchen getting on with some work, I had my headphones on, but my God, they were really going at it that day, big old squeals and knocks, as if they had set up a little wrestling ring down there, I could hear it even over my music. I take my headphones off and listen. I try to see how many I can hear but it's difficult. Three maybe? I decide to investigate. I follow the noise over to the washing machine. I crouch down to have a look under the counter but I can't get low enough to see properly. I lie flat on my stomach and I can smell them, a kind of heavy, sweaty musk. Smell them, but not see them... Billy'll be back soon – he'll think I've gone mad, I better put the kitchen back together... Just then – movement! At the back, just to the left of the washing machine there's a small hole in the brick where a pipe passes through to the outside world, and there it is, a nose, whiskers. I stay completely still, if I move even a tiny bit it'll see me and run off. The head passes through the hole, and now it's squeezing itself out, and it's struggling. There's the head, there we go, one last push, nearly there. And this great big thing drops to the floor and just sits there. (*beat*) There's something so human about it. It's looking me right in the eyes. It's not even scared, it just looks surprised. I lay there, she sat there, our eyes locked together for what felt like an age. There's a cheekiness about her, but also innocence. There's sadness, too. Real, human emotion. She's a little life. (*beat*) I wonder whether maybe, just maybe, she's reading as much into me as I am into her. I don't know what made me, but in that moment I slowly, ever so slowly tip-toed with my fingers towards her. She takes a small step back, and then carefully, measuredly, steps up onto my hand, using my fingers as little stairs, and she walks along my arm towards my neck. I remember seeing films where petrified housewives would leap up onto chairs and scream at even the smallest mouse. Is this what they were frightened of? This happy little thing? Her hairs are brushing against mine now, she's having a good inspection, she rubs her cheek against my lower lip, perhaps relieving an itch. I can smell her clearly now, her little ears are flopping against my nostrils, there's a sweetness to that smell, almost sickly. She's tender in the way she touches me, in some strange way, it feels like I know her. Our eyes meet again. (*pause*) Alice? Keys in the front door, it opens –

BILLY: She told me what had happened.

RACHEL: He wasn't best pleased.

BILLY: They carry the fucking plague, Rach, what were you thinking?

RACHEL: It was cute.

BILLY: I'll tell you what aren't cute-

RACHEL: What?

BILLY: Buboes.

RACHEL: What's that?

BILLY: It's what you get from rats. Big black swollen bulbs of pus in your armpits and all over your fanny.

RACHEL: That's disgusting.

BILLY: Exactly. Rats are disgusting. Don't touch them, OK? I heard a story about a boy who fell over in rat piss and went blind.

RACHEL: Is that true?

BILLY: I don't know. But I don't really care to find out. Shower. Now.

RACHEL: And life continued.

BILLY: As did the scratching.

RACHEL: I got used to it.

BILLY: I didn't. It would keep me up at night.

RACHEL: They'd moved into the bedroom walls.

BILLY: One of them was stuck in the wall between our bedrooms.

RACHEL: It started to get between us. One night I get woken up at four AM by a scream.

BILLY: It was torture. Sleep deprivation, they literally use that as torture.

RACHEL: Babe, what the fuck are you screaming about?

BILLY: The fucking scratching. It won't stop- it won't fucking stop!

RACHEL: Hey, hey, calm down, it's OK-

BILLY: It's not OK, how am I supposed to sleep?

RACHEL: We can switch for the night, maybe it's quieter in my room, I can-

BILLY: It's not fucking quieter, it's just you sleep like the fucking dead, please, please, just leave me alone.

RACHEL: Babe –

BILLY: Leave.

RACHEL: OK, but please don't scream, Bill, because it really freaked me out just then.

BILLY: I just want to sleep.

RACHEL: Yeah, well you're not the only one!

BILLY: The next day I bought an airgun.

RACHEL: I thought that was too far.

BILLY: A big old rifle style one.

RACHEL: Quite a bit too far actually.

BILLY: I was in the kitchen

RACHEL: I was in bed.

BILLY: I was sat cross-legged on the kitchen table with the rifle pointed at the hole where Rachel saw the last one.

RACHEL: I was doing some research, turns out most rats actually don't carry diseases that can be contracted by humans, apparently they're capable of love, and make great pets.

BILLY: I hear something.

RACHEL: I hear something.

BILLY: Scratching.

RACHEL: Scratching.

BILLY: Under the counter.

RACHEL: In the wall.

BILLY: I don't move a muscle.

RACHEL: I climb out of bed.

BILLY: I press the gun against my shoulder and line up my sights.

RACHEL: I drag my cupboard a few inches away from the wall and press my cheek flat against it to look behind.

BILLY: Movement.

RACHEL: Movement.

BILLY: Black shapes in the darkness.

RACHEL: Flaking plaster, being pushed outwards.

BILLY: Like shadows of shadows.

RACHEL: Like the hatching egg from that scene in Jurassic Park.

BILLY: I feel the weight of the trigger pushing back against my finger.

RACHEL: I crouch down. I can hear it sucking in the air. Tasting freedom.

BILLY: It's only a matter of time.

RACHEL: Here it comes.

BILLY: There it is.

RACHEL: I push away loose parts of the wall and it struggles through the hole and plops onto the floor.

BILLY: I track it as it creeps past the dishwasher towards the bin. No clear shot. It has to be still. It climbs up the side of the bin and drops inside, rustling about. Now it's just a waiting game.

RACHEL: I don't want to scare it away. It's all white because it's coated in dust from the loose plaster. I lay down my hand like I did with the first one.

BILLY: It's head pops back out of the bin, Rach had moussaka for dinner and it's carrying some of the scraps in its mouth.

RACHEL: And sure as anything, with no hesitation, it jumps up.

BILLY: It pauses half way to the counter when some of the food falls to the floor.

RACHEL: I stroke it, it hooks it's claws into my jumper and in one big leap jumps up onto my shoulder.

BILLY: Bingo. I squeeze the trigger.

RACHEL: I turn my head to face it, it's right by my mouth, don't ask me why but in that moment it was so sweet, so interested. I kissed it.

BOTH: Bang!

RACHEL: It starts at the noise and so do I.

BILLY: A direct hit. Right in the middle. It's squirming on the floor.

RACHEL: We stand up.

BILLY: I hop down.

RACHEL: Make for the door.

BILLY: And I stamp on its head. A noise from the corridor.

RACHEL: What the fuck are you doing?

BILLY: I got it! I fucking got it!

RACHEL: Have you completely lost your mind?

BILLY: Rachel –

RACHEL: It's one in the morning!

BILLY: Rach, don't move. Don't fucking move.

RACHEL: Don't point that fucking gun at me.

BILLY: Don't –

RACHEL: Bill – what are you-?

BILLY: It's on your shoulder.

RACHEL: I know!

BOTH: Bang!

RACHEL: (*screams*) Fuck!

BILLY: Shit.

RACHEL: You shot me!

BILLY: Oh my God, I'm so sorry babe.

RACHEL: You fucking shot me. I'm bleeding.

(*Beat*)

BILLY: I know it's bad, but I could only focus on the rat. It jumped off her shoulder a scuttled past back where the other one had come from.

RACHEL: Bill!

BILLY: I'm sorry! I wasn't aiming for you. It's not a real bullet, it's just an airgun.

RACHEL: I need to go to the hospital.

BILLY: Don't be silly.

RACHEL: It's stuck in me, the bullet-

BILLY: It's not a bullet, it's only a pellet.

RACHEL: Well it still fucking hurts!

BILLY: Let's have a look.

RACHEL: Get away from me!

BILLY: Fine! Fine, go to the hospital, and you can blame it all on me.

RACHEL: Well who else is to blame you fucking PSYCHOPATH!?

(*Pause*)

BILLY: I put the gun away in the cellar after that.

RACHEL: I didn't go to the hospital in the end.

BILLY: We talked about it –

RACHEL: He guilt tripped me.

BILLY: It just made sense not to-

RACHEL: It was classic gaslighting-

BILLY: We agreed it would be better to just-

RACHEL: He pulled out the bullet-

BILLY: Pellet –

RACHEL: With a pair of tweezers.

BILLY: I was very precise about it.

RACHEL: It hurt like a bitch.

BILLY: Maybe in a past life I was a surgeon-

RACHEL: Or a complete dickhead, perhaps.

(*Pause*)

I'm out shopping the next day, arm all bandaged up. Food shopping, not shopping shopping, and on the way home from Morrison's I take a little detour. I kind of knew what I was doing, but it didn't feel like a conscious choice to go a different route, something subliminal was driving me, I think. I stop outside a little pet shop about a ten minute walk from ours and look in through the window. There's a bored looking old bloke leaning on the counter. Little pointy white beard and quite long silver hair. He was like a cross between Rolf Harris and Billy Connolly. I walk in and the little bells above the door go ding-ding. He looks over surprised. Bill can you be the guy?

BILLY: Me?

RACHEL: No, the other Bill. Yes, you.

BILLY: I can try.

RACHEL: Makes the story better, doesn't it.

BILLY: OK, sure.

RACHEL: You remember how it goes?

BILLY: Yeah, I think so.

RACHEL: You start.

BILLY: We don't normally get customers this time on a Monday.

RACHEL: He was Welsh.

BILLY: We don't normally get customers this time on a Monday.

RACHEL: Welsh, Bill, not Pakistani.

BILLY: I'll just do it in my own voice.

RACHEL: Fine, whatever, but he was Welsh. Go again.

BILLY: We don't normally get customers this time on a Monday.

RACHEL: It's a Tuesday.

BILLY: We don't normally get customers this time on a Tuesday.

RACHEL: No, that's what I said.

BILLY: What?

RACHEL: I said "It's a Tuesday", and he goes, *So it is, I lose track in the week, nothing in here to remind you what day it is.*

BILLY: Wow.

RACHEL: What?

BILLY: That's a really good Welsh accent.

RACHEL: We can swap if you want.

BILLY: That would be confusing, we've started now.

RACHEL: Yeah, to be honest, you're ruining my story.

BILLY: Me?

RACHEL: Yes.

BILLY: Shall we start again?

RACHEL: Forget it, Bill. Sorry I even asked. So anyway he says that and then I notice behind him. Small cages. Above them is a hand written sign that says "rodents".

Looking at my rodents are you? We've got hamsters, guinea pigs, door mice, field mice and one little house mouse; rats in black, blue and dumbo sphinx.

Can I take a look?

He nods and leads me behind the counter.

Suddenly there's movement in some of the cages.

The rat cages.

They all stop what they're doing and hurry over to the side closest to me.

Bloody hell! They like you.

I chuckled back politely and said

Looks like it, doesn't it...? Are they OK in there?

OK? What do you mean?

In the cages.

We look after them well in here.

Yeah I suppose so.

But their little eyes were screaming. They'd come over because they knew I would understand, because they knew I was their salvation.

I'll take all of them.

But there are over thirty in here.

I know.

You'll need a lot of space, a lot of cages.

I won't keep them in cages.

They'll go feral, you know.

I'll take care of them. Is there a problem?

It's just... I want to make sure they find a good home, that they're well looked after. I walk over to a cage containing three black rats and undo the latch on the door.

The rats clamber over each other to get out, they scramble out of the door, up my arm, one sits on my right shoulder, another on my left and the third clings onto the front of my jumper.

The look on his face.

BILLY: All day I'd been thinking about the airgun incident. Well, not so much the airgun bit, but the stamp. When I squashed its head. How the back half of its body twitched a few times, and its tail flickered in a crescent motion for a couple of seconds before the nervous system shut down and it stopped. That day I'd set up a new kind of trap, something I'd seen on YouTube. You fill a bucket half way with water then you set up a platform over the bucket with a bit of food on it. I look in the fridge. He liked the moussaka, that last one. I fucking hate moussaka personally, but then the only thing I actually do like is chicken nuggets. And chips. With a cheesecake for pudding. It's the OCD. The nuggets are mine anyway, I grab the moussaka. Anyway, the idea is that when the rat sets foot on the platform it collapses and in he goes, into the bucket where he eventually drowns. When I got back Rach was out –

RACHEL: I'd taken the car out to the pet shop to pick up the –

BILLY: This is my bit. Anyway, she was out, and the first thing I did was check the bucket for any dead. I'd caught something. But it wasn't dead. It was standing there in the bucket, its head above the waterline looking fed up. I reached in, down into the water, and picked it up by its tail. I hold it up in front of me, it's all bedraggled and wriggling about, soaking wet, looking like a drowned rat, but less drowned. I spin it around by it's tail and it flicks a line of water droplets up the wall, across the ceiling, and back down the other wall. Satisfying. It starts yelping and squealing. I felt this adrenaline rush. It was like being a kid again. All those memories of killing animals as a boy, and enjoying it, all those feelings came back, the feeling of total power. In a split second a million ways I could murder it came flooding into my head. No. Come on, Bill. Getting rid of the rats is a job. You're not supposed to enjoy it. Make it quick. I went to the drawer and pulled out a hammer. I held down the rat on a chopping board with my left hand and quickly brought the hammer down on it's head. I couldn't help feeling it was a waste, though. Don't get me wrong, it felt good. It felt even better than the stamp in a way, because I had time to really think about what I was doing. But it did also feel like a waste. Like I could have done something more enjoyable, make it last a bit longer. Just then I heard the car pull up outside. Rachel can't see this, she'll go berserk. I tip the rat into the bin and cover it up with some food packaging. I quickly rinse the chopping board and shove it in the dishwasher. The front door opens, I put the hammer behind my back.

Hi love!

RACHEL: Hey Bill, now don't be angry –

BILLY: Angry about what?

RACHEL: Well I – What have you got behind your back.

BILLY: Hammer.

RACHEL: Why?

BILLY: I was just fixing the, er –

RACHEL: I've –

BILLY: The sideboard. Loose nail.

RACHEL: I've bought some pets.

BILLY: There was a – pets?

RACHEL: Pets.

BILLY: What kind of pets?

RACHEL: You're going to think I've lost the plot.

BILLY: We don't need pets.

RACHEL: Come and have a look.

BILLY: She leads me out to the car, up to the window, and I look in and the car is crawling with them.

RACHEL: Rats, Bill.

BILLY: What the fuck is this, some kind of joke?

RACHEL: Don't you think they're cute?

BILLY: What the fuck?

RACHEL: Look, they really like me.

BILLY: She opens the back door and they all come rushing over, out on to the street. They one by one climb up her legs and they make perches on her, like birds on a scarecrow.

RACHEL: Look.

BILLY: I'm gonna be sick.

RACHEL: Here, hold one.

BILLY: Get the fuck away from me with those things.

RACHEL: They're pets, Bill, they aren't wild like the ones in the house, they're clean.

BILLY: I don't care, you're taking them back. Now.

RACHEL: I'm not, Bill.

BILLY: You are. Get back in the car, right now –

RACHEL: No –

BILLY: And drive them back to the pet shop –

RACHEL: No –

BILLY: Fine then, I'll do it. And I reach for one and then –

RACHEL: (*short, harsh, loud*) NO!

(*Pause*)

BILLY: And the rats. They all turned to look at me, screeching and baring their teeth. I back off. Curtains twitch all down the street.

RACHEL: They're mine. Not yours. They'll stay in my room, and if you even think about touching them I'll kill you. Do you understand?

BILLY: Still staring at me, she gestures with her hand to the front door, which is still resting open. The rats, one by one, climb down off her and form a single file line in through the door and left, into her bedroom. She turns around and follows them in. I stood in the street, heart racing for what felt like an hour. When I get in she's in her bedroom with the door closed and I can hear her talking to them. The way she speaks, it's as if they're having a conversation, as if she's replying to questions they've asked her. I stand there listening for a while and then I sit in the kitchen and spend the rest of the night alone with the scratching.

RACHEL: The next morning my mum's carer calls me, she's unwell so I decide to pay her a visit. I lock my bedroom door on the way out of the house and leave without saying goodbye to Bill.

BILLY: I take up my usual spot on the sofa and try to distract myself with a bit of light hearted daytime TV. The Hairy Bikers, I think it was, but I can't concentrate. The living room wall backs on to her bedroom and all I can think about is them, just the other side of the wall. I knew she was weird, we both have our quirks, but this… It was like something had changed in her overnight. Maybe we rushed into things. Maybe we should have lived together a while before choosing to get married.

Maybe I should skin one. What? Where did that come from? It's a part of my OCD. Now, I don't wanna blame everything on the OCD, but intrusive thoughts. I get obsessive about certain tasks, that's the part people know about but the part people don't mention so often is the intrusive thoughts. A good example would be imagine you're standing on the tube platform waiting for a train, and there are a bunch of other people waiting with you. And suddenly a thought comes into your head, a thought you really shouldn't be thinking, a thought of pushing someone onto the tracks. Maybe you've experienced it. It's one of the more common ones for some reason. And you curse yourself for even thinking about it, but then all you can think about is that you thought about it, and the thought grows stronger and stronger until it feels like you're just gonna do it. Without even thinking about it, like a knee-jerk reaction to your own thoughts. That's how it feels for me, a lot of the time. I mean, I can control them, obviously, otherwise I'd be in prison. I'd never actually do that. Maybe I should cut one open and remove its insides while it's still alive, they used to do that in the old days with people, didn't they? Hanged, drawn and quartered. Maybe that would be fun. For fuck's sake, no Bill. But it would be fun, wouldn't it? I've got to do it, I've just got to do it. But she said she would kill me if I touched them, and the look in her eyes. I can't.

In the car.

Engine on.

Pet shop door.

Ding-ding.

They'd restocked. They had twenty-three black rats and I bought the lot. Took them away in cages and unloaded them into my bedroom.

What now?

I sit on the edge of my bed and watch them.

They're disgusting.

They crawl all over each other shitting and squeaking with their long, wiry tails bumping against each other.

I clear everything off my desk and move one of the cages up onto it.

I pull up my wheelie chair and sit there staring at them.

The stink of them.

Not as bad as the ones under the kitchen but the same thick musk that makes you want to puke.

She has hers, I have mine. I can do what I want with these ones.

I grab the keys to my shed and head into the garden.

The shed is like Aladdin's cave.

It took me back to the cat. To the decision, which weapon, only this time I was in no rush. That feeling, it was suppressed for so long, but now here it was again and even more exciting. It was like acting out a fetish you'd had hibernating in you for years, but never thought would actually happen. A sordid, guilty kind of excitement. The next three hours are a bit of a blur. I skinned them, beheaded them, blinded them, dropped them in acid, cut their tails off, fed them to each other, beat them, chopped them in half, drilled through them, nailed them to the wall, put them in the microwave, ground them into a paste. It was a bloodbath. It was the most thrilling thing I had ever experienced. But now it was over. I sat there breathing hard. I tried to make myself a cup of tea but my hands were shaking too much. I wanted more. I walked over to the door of Rach's bedroom. I grip the handle and turn. Locked. She's taken the key with her. I can hear them through the door. How long do you think she'll be out? No. No. That's insane. I go to the living room and sit on the sofa and stare out the window and try to think about something – anything – else. But the thought is already there, it's already taken over.

RACHEL: I'm in the car on the way home, Mum was OK, just a bit poorly, but at her age it's easy to see why the carer gets panicked. It's been hard to concentrate on her knowing that Bill's at home alone with my babies. I can't help imagining that he's hurt them, or taken them back to the pet shop. When I get in, the house feels eerie.

Billy?

Bill?

Nothing.

He must be out.

I step towards my bedroom door, and I stop. That's when I see. The door is not locked any more.

It's swaying in a draft coming through from where the back door has been left open.

Another step.

The wood on the lock side of the door is splintered and cracked.

It's been forced open. What's in there? What has he done? Another.

(*Pause*)

BILLY: It started with a spot.

RACHEL: Just a little spot, no bigger than a fingertip.

BILLY: I was in my room watching some Netflix.

RACHEL: This is going back a bit.

BILLY: Just a couple of days after we moved in.

RACHEL: We still had half our stuff in boxes.

BILLY: We were still devastatingly in love.

RACHEL: I remember waddling out the toilet door with my knickers around my ankles and my toothbrush sticking out my mouth, peering round at him. He looked at me and laughed, he said I looked like a... something, he said I looked like something funny, and turned back to the screen. A baby. That's what he said I looked like.

There's a spot here.

BILLY: A spot where?

RACHEL: Here, Bill, on my fucking pants.

BILLY: Well what does that mean?

RACHEL: I don't know.

BILLY: Is it... Is it happening?

RACHEL: Bill was suddenly alert. I wasn't feeling any of the tell-tale signs, I wasn't feeling anything at all... I don't think so.

BILLY: Well that's... good, that's definitely good, that would be too soon, right? Tell you what, I'll drive you over to the clinic tomorrow morning. If you feel anything sooner, tell me and we'll go to hospital tonight, alright babe?

RACHEL: I love you, Bill.

BILLY: I love you too, Rach. Night.

RACHEL: I woke up the next morning with a little bit of pain, not much, just a little bit. I had no idea what to expect from all this really, other than words I'd read in books and from watching One Born Every Minute. I didn't know for sure but my gut was telling me she was on the way.

I nudged Billy and told him to get a coffee on, he said fine and that we should probably get going if it really was happening now.

I remember being surprised by how easy it was, how ready I felt. This was it, this had to be it.

I'm at the doctor's now and I've got half my kit off, top up to my tits, belly out, fanny out. Bill's sitting there, he doesn't know which way to look, doctor's got his rubber gloves on, he's having a good old feel.

BILLY: *So this pain*

RACHEL: Said the doctor

BILLY: *When did it start?*

RACHEL: This morning.

BILLY: *Before or after the spot of blood?*

RACHEL: After, the spot was last night.

BILLY: *OK, and is the pain coming in waves, or is it more a constant ache?*

RACHEL: Umm, I don't know, it's kind of like an ache but yeah it comes in waves.

BILLY: *No sharp pains then?*

RACHEL: No, none of that.

BILLY: *OK.*

RACHEL: He said that with a kind of chirpiness in his voice, like, "well that's alright then". I looked round at Billy and he gave me a little wink.

Doctor reaches round for his listening machine and comes back to me.

BILLY: *I'm going to feel for the heartbeat, just check she's all OK in there.*

RACHEL: We thought I might be going into labour, am I not?

BILLY: *Please don't talk.*

RACHEL: He said, listening intently to my tummy.

Bill pipes up

BILLY: I was born four weeks early, you know, apparently I was only the size of a –

RACHEL: Shut up, Bill.

We're in silence now, it's kind of awkward. Billy's just staring at this diagram of the womb that's on the wall, and I'm just staring at Billy. He's so much better at being annoying than actually helping me get through all this. And the silence went on and on forever.

At some point the silence changed. It was a nervous silence now.

What's going on down there?

BILLY: *I'm not... I'm not finding her at the moment.*

RACHEL: She's probably hiding somewhere in there, look at the fucking size of me, there's enough space.

BILLY: *Be quiet.*

RACHEL: He said

BILLY: More silence.

I'm going to do an ultrasound, just stay where you are, I'll be right back.

So he goes off for a minute and the silence continues, it's changed again, this time from a nervous silence to a breathless one.

RACHEL: Billy broke it first.

BILLY: I don't understand why he can't just fucking tell us what's going on.

RACHEL: Shut up, Bill, he's doing his job.

He comes back in the room at this moment and splodges a load of that jelly stuff on me. He gets the machine up and running and gets to work.

BILLY: There she is,

RACHEL: Bill pointed at the screen.

There she was. It was like a wave of utter relief. I let out a little laugh. There she was. Our girl, all curled up inside me.

But the doctor wasn't laughing. In fact, his face had gone all stiff and twisted up at the edges.

What's wrong?

BILLY: *It's, umm.*

RACHEL: Seriously, what's wrong?

Billy stands up and his voice is doing that thing it does before he kicks off, it's all shaky and weak.

BILLY: Why won't you tell us?

RACHEL: He tells Billy to sit down. He can't even look us in the eye. He says he isn't getting a heartbeat.

(*Beat*)

BILLY: Well what does that mean?

RACHEL: But we knew what it meant. Everyone knows what that means. And that's the exact moment the bottom of my world fell off and everything came pouring out. All the joy, the excitement, the love, the trust, the fear, the nerves. It all just fell away onto the floor of the clinic.

Three days.

That's how long I had to keep carrying my girl inside me after that.

And you know.

You know that the doctor... is a doctor, he wouldn't make a mistake that huge. But somewhere in me I think I had a glimmer of hope left, somewhere near my heart, that still hadn't fallen out of me.

Three days can be a really long time, you know.

And then there was the drive to the hospital, it seemed to go on forever, to deliver the...

(*Rachel stifles what could have been a flood of tears*)

They put you in the same ward as the others, did you know that?

I didn't.

But they do.

That late on in the pregnancy, they stick you in with all the others to deliver the baby.

And I pushed, and I pushed, and I shat myself, and I tore parts of me I never even knew I had, and I wouldn't take the drugs, I just pushed, and screamed and turned my knuckles white and said that thing they always said you would say. I can't do this anymore. But I did, I struggled through it, and I heard the nurses, here's the head, there we go, one last push, nearly there...

And then it was done.

And they held up my little girl.

And she was alive.

She was.

So perfect, and covered in muck, and so completely new to the world.

She was the most beautiful thing I'd ever seen.

She was.

And then I heard the cry.

You don't hear babies cry the same after childbirth.

It cut right through me.

But it wasn't her cry.

It was one of a million cries ringing out all around the ward. They filled up my head.

But none of them were hers.

And I remember willing her, you know, willing her with everything.

Go on. You can do it. Just cry, just once, just for a second.

Billy was there next to me, gripping onto my arm, looking down at the floor. We may as well have been on different planets.

And they carried her away.

And I watched as they did.

(*Pause*)

> So when I turned the corner into my room, and I saw the blood on the wall, and I saw the death, and I saw the chaos, and severed heads, all stuck on toothpicks, all staring at me. And I saw the way my babies, all of them, were massacred, I saw the spot again, no bigger than a fingertip.
>
> I know how it sounds. I know.
>
> But you don't understand.
>
> You weren't there.
>
> Rat's aren't supposed to love a human that way.
>
> And so even though I knew I shouldn't love them like I did, I couldn't help it. Because my girl was in them.

(*Silence. When they speak, their voices are barely above a whisper*)

BILLY: Rach, I –

RACHEL: Don't.

(*Pause*)

BILLY: It wasn't –

RACHEL: Don't speak.

(*Beat*)

BILLY: There are more in the car, babe.

RACHEL: Were you going to kill them too?

(*Pause*)

BILLY: They're vermin, Rach.

(*Pause*)

RACHEL: You don't see it.

BILLY: Don't see what?

RACHEL: Just because you don't see it, it doesn't mean she isn't in there.

BILLY: What am I not seeing babe?

RACHEL: You don't understand –

BILLY: Then make me understand.

RACHEL: Her.

BILLY: Her?

(*Pause*)

RACHEL: The first time I saw one, in the kitchen, it wasn't afraid, she climbed up my arm.

BILLY: What are you talking about?

RACHEL: She looked into my eyes, and I saw her.

BILLY: Saw who?

RACHEL: You know who I'm talking about.

BILLY: No –

RACHEL: Alice.

BILLY: No –

RACHEL: Yes.

BILLY: Don't say her name, babe.

RACHEL: It was Alice.

BILLY: Please. (*Billy is crying, Rachel moves over and hugs him*)

RACHEL: Not mentioning her, never talking about her, it doesn't make what happened any less real. The important thing is she's back, Billy. I know what I saw – felt – I know what I felt.

BILLY: Listen to me Rach,

RACHEL: She is. You've seen the way they act around me. That isn't what rats do, I know you know that. She's back.

(*Pause*)

BILLY: We've been having problems recently, and I know a lot of that's my fault, I've got this compulsion, and I – and I know it's wrong, and I know it's bad and I've been trying to fight it, these… urges… I've been having, but I haven't been doing very well and I'm worried that I've got a problem, it's hard because we've clearly both been going through a lot, and maybe I haven't – no – no – I haven't been giving you the attention you deserve but you have to understand how this sounds. She died, Rachel. We both saw her.

RACHEL: I know that.

BILLY: She's gone, Rach.

RACHEL: (*Resolute*) She isn't gone.

(*Pause*)

BILLY: Rach and I agreed we both needed some space to get our heads in order. The urge to kill had subsided, I –

RACHEL: He had –

BILLY: Do you mind? Would you please stop interrupting me when it's my fucking bit?

RACHEL: We're supposed to be doing this together.

BILLY: Can I carry on?

RACHEL: There's no need to be rude.

BILLY: Sorry about her. Where was I? I took the cages from the –

RACHEL: You've done that bit.

BILLY: Fine, you fucking do it.

(*Pause*)

BILLY: You can't can you? Because you don't know the lines, because it's my bit.

RACHEL: Honestly, I'm gonna leave in a minute if you don't change your tone.

BILLY: I took the cages from the car and left them in the corridor, stacked up. Rach and I agreed we both needed –

RACHEL: Ugh.

BILLY: What? What? This is embarrassing. We both needed some space to get our heads in order. The urge to kill had subsided, I had promised myself I wouldn't do it any more, that I'd find a way to control it even when it felt impossible. I started looking at self-help class – I can feel you there.

RACHEL: What?

BILLY: Looking at me, your eyes are boring into me.

RACHEL: What, I can't look at you now?

BILLY: We said we wouldn't do this –

RACHEL: Do what, I'm not doing –

BILLY: Have a domestic. Here. In front of them.

(*Beat*)

RACHEL: He had left the room as it was, in a state of chaos. I went for a long walk and when I came back the worst of it was gone. But the smell was still there and the bloodstains on the walls almost looked worse where he had tried to clean them off.

BILLY: Why rats?

RACHEL: His bedroom door was closed and I could hear him in there, I went through to the kitchen and saw the shed was still unlocked. I went to lock it and when I looked through the open door I saw everything he had used. Knives, pins, hammers, all still coated in a film of blood. On a shelf near the door were boxes of rat poison.

BILLY: Why not a dolphin? Or a lion or something, or even just another person? I mean I get it, the whole reincarnation thing. None of us know what happens after you die so anyone's guess is as good as mine, but why would she have been brought back as rats? She was innocent, she never even drew a breath.

RACHEL: I picked up the box on top and opened it up. I was like a blue gel wrapped tightly in clear plastic. I ignored the warning on the packet and tore open one of the sachets. It smelled sweet.

BILLY: Why not be brought back as a house cat or something, fed well, a good life, freedom to do whatever she wanted? Or a bird or... Anything, surely, almost anything is better than a rat.

RACHEL: I locked up the shed and took some food to the rats left in the car. They could stay in there for a while, they'd at least be safe in there.

BILLY: What if she was right?

(*Pause*)

I want to work on myself. I remember I said that to her once, a long time ago. You make me want to be a better man.

RACHEL: You're already perfect –

BILLY: Believe me, I'm not babe.

RACHEL: Well you're perfect for me, then.

BILLY: That was back then, but things had changed, I had changed.

RACHEL: Do you wanna put that thing away?

BILLY: It's a book.

RACHEL: I can see it's a book, it's dinner time Bill, can't you –

BILLY: I got it on Amazon.

RACHEL: Great.

BILLY: It's by Vikram Balakrishnan.

RACHEL: Finished with your nuggets?

BILLY: Yeah, thanks love. It's self-help, I really think it's working.

RACHEL: What page you on?

BILLY: Page… Ten. He uses changing a lightbulb as an analogy for making changes deep within.

RACHEL: Cheesecake?

BILLY: Yes please, babe. It says here when you change a bulb you might have to stand on a chair, which is supposed to represent not being afraid to ask for help, so I guess the chair is you. It's all very proverbial.

RACHEL: I think it's great you're taking this seriously, Bill.

BILLY: Well I – Why's the cake blue?

RACHEL: Blueberries, don't you like it?

BILLY: Haven't tried it yet... Delicious, babe. Next it says the lightbulb is gonna be hot, of course, so you have to wait for it to cool down.

RACHEL: Sounds like bollocks to me.

BILLY: Well that's great then.

RACHEL: What?

BILLY: I'm doing this for you!

RACHEL: You're doing self-help for me?

BILLY: Yes! – Where are you going?

RACHEL: To the car. They need feeding.

BILLY: Things did seem better. Far from perfect, but on the mend, perhaps. Turns out the space we had agreed we needed was more for her. She spent half her time in the car and half her time in the house, but when we were together we were both making an effort, doing the right things to try and stitch the tatters of our relationship back together. I'd do things, nice things, I'd go out of my way to show her I really meant what I was doing and she would just cook for me, relentlessly. Nuggets, chips and her new blueberry cheesecake for every meal. That's what love is all about. Not because love relies on chicken nuggets, just because she knows me, and she wanted me to see that, I think.

What do you think?

RACHEL: They're very colourful.

BILLY: Ponies.

RACHEL: Ponies?

BILLY: They're the big ones. These ones are roses, the tall ones are called snapdragons – the leafy things are... erm –

RACHEL: Peonies, Bill, they're called peonies, not ponies.

BILLY: Do you like them? They're for you.

RACHEL: They're nice.

BILLY: I've ordered a subscription, a new bouquet every week, I know how much you like flowers.

RACHEL: You've never done this before.

BILLY: Well I'm starting now, never too late to –

RACHEL: You OK Bill? You're looking a bit peaky.

BILLY: I'm fine.

(*Beat*)

RACHEL: You sure?

BILLY: Yeah, I'm sure.

RACHEL: 'Cos I know what you're like, if it's a cold it's death and if it's death there's nothing wrong.

BILLY: I have had a bit of a funny stomach.

RACHEL: You're sweating.

BILLY: Am I?

RACHEL: Touch your forehead... Maybe you should have a lie down.

BILLY: No, no, I'm fine. I need to sort the garden out anyway. But there you go... flowers.

RACHEL: Thank you.

(*Pause*)

BILLY: Rach was right. I wasn't exactly on top form. I battled it for as long as I could but the slight sickness in my stomach turned to cramps and my head started feeling funny. After twenty-five minutes outside sweating over cut grass and refuse sacks I headed back in and made a beeline for the sofa.

RACHEL: Babe, seriously, are you OK?

BILLY: I'm fine.

RACHEL: Can I get you anything?

BILLY: No, I just need to sleep it off, it's nothing.

RACHEL: Nothing. Right. Well when you wake up I've still got three-quarters of that cheesecake. Special treat for a sick boy. Sound OK?

BILLY: That sounds amazing Rach. I love you, you know that.

RACHEL: And some chicken nuggets for whenever you can stomach them.

BILLY: I'm sorry.

RACHEL: Sorry for what?

BILLY: For being like this.

RACHEL: Like what?

BILLY: Sick.

(*Pause*)

RACHEL: Don't be stupid.

(*Beat*)

BILLY: Jump to four days later and I'm still there sprawled out across the sofa, I've barely moved other than to piss and everything hurts… especially the pissing. Rach has been a fucking godsend, as always. At first it felt like this was bringing us closer together. Now I was just fucked.

Do you think I should go to hospital?

RACHEL: You're through the worst of it Bill, what are they gonna do for you any better than I will here? All you've gots a fever. Anyway, you know what these hospitals are like at the moment. It's all masks and gowns and they wouldn't even let me in to see you... you're better off here where I can take proper care of you, feed you what you like.

(*Billy clutches at his face. There's blood*)

What's up?

BILLY: Nosebleed.

RACHEL: What, again?

BILLY: I dunno what's wrong with me.

RACHEL: How many's that?

BILLY: I dunno, four, I think.

(*Billy whimpers into a weep*)

BILLY: I don't think I'm very well.

RACHEL: Sh-sh. Come here.

(*As Billy speaks blood comes bubbling out of his mouth*)

BILLY: I think I need to go to the –

RACHEL: Oh my God, babe.

(*Billy wretches and more blood comes out of his mouth, he coughs, splutters and wipes his face, spreading it all over himself*)

BILLY: Can you help me go to the toilet?

RACHEL: Here we go, take my arm, let's get you up, two, three.

BILLY: I love you so much. (*Exit Billy*)

(*Pause*)

RACHEL: It was all over quicker than I expected. After a day of nosebleeds, coughing and vomiting up blood, it was game over. I'd help him to the toilet and there would be spots of it on the sofa, it was leaking out of his cock. He was pissing, shitting the stuff. Eventually it started coming out his eyes, and the best thing? It just wouldn't stop. Brodifacoum. It's a funny kind of word, I don't even know if that's how it's pronounced properly, but that's the stuff. Rat poison. It thins your blood, stops it from clotting, your life source comes pouring out your every orifice, relentlessly. When he finally died it was coming out of his pores. He passed in a blood-soaked hole on the sofa, pale as a ghost with a million tiny orbs of blood oozing out his skin. I went out to the car and I brought my babies back into the house. The cellar was dark so I grabbed the torch from Billy's shed and tried the switch. Nothing. Into the blackness.

I'm feeling my way around. I know it's in here.

I feel dust on my fingertips as I move my hands over boxes of still unpacked items from the move-in.

Something cold. Metal. I run my hand down it until I feel the wood, a trigger. I take it up, and feel my way back to the steps upstairs.

My babies are all over the ground floor, running about, settling in to their new home.

They'll be here long after both of us are gone. They'll fuck it out like animals, they'll multiply and multiply until there are thousands, and she'll be in every one of them. More life than she would ever have had if things hadn't been the way they were. And they'll fight over our bodies until there's nothing left of us but bones.

I raise the barrel of the air rifle to my eye and hope for the best.

Maybe this has saved me.

I think of the man on the tracks. How easy he made it look.

There was still a smile on his face as he raced across the platform. I take a breath and look down the corridor.

There she is.

She's watching me through all those little eyes.

I see in her eyes the same thrill we had as we stared on from the train window all that time ago.

I give her a smile.

(*Rachel takes a deep breath, BLACKOUT*)

END